# WOW

## YOUR WAY INTO THE JOB

## OF YOUR DREAMS

# WOW

## YOUR WAY INTO THE JOB
## OF YOUR DREAMS

Frances Cole Jones

978-1-4976-4949-1

Distributed by Open Road Distribution
345 Hudson Street
New York, NY 10014
www.openroadmedia.com

# TABLE OF CONTENTS

# TABLE OF CONTENTS

# INTRODUCTION

You're smart.

You're self-aware.

You have a lot to offer.

So you might be wondering if you really need this book.

I'm here to tell you that the reasons above are precisely why you do. Because like every one of the clients I've coached into the job of their dreams, you know that it's what you *don't* yet know that can make all the difference in whether you land or lose that coveted job.

They are looking for the edge that will set them apart. I'm here to give it to you.

What I'm not here to do is to tell you what your dream job is, or even to help you figure that out. Suffice to say it's whatever position, industry, or exciting idea you have about your next career move. Instead, I'm here to help you take all your skills, smarts, and willingness to learn and transform that vision into a reality.

By the time you finish reading this book, you'll have the edge you need to set yourself apart from even the toughest competitor.

A little bit about me:

I've been coaching people into their dream jobs for the last sixteen years. From students fresh out of college with zero idea how to navigate the job market, to mothers seeking to return to the work force and concerned about having viable skill sets, to Young Turks from Wall Street who were let go in the last few years of recession and want to get back in the game, to captains of industry seeking to find a better fit for their highly refined skills and broad range of interests, I have helped them all.

Regardless of what your concern might be: that you don't have the requisite experience, that you have a gap in your resume, that you've been let go from previous jobs, that you're too qualified, too old, too young, too *frustrated* to keep looking for that dream job, I promise you I can help.

Over the years I've been coaching, I'm proud to say that

99.9% of my clients have found their way into their dream jobs. Does it sometimes require a sophisticated strategy? Yes. Are there moments where everyone is pulling out their hair? You bet. Is it in any way easy/effortless/fun? Sometimes—but mostly it's hard work.

Most importantly, do my clients land the jobs of their dreams?

Yes, they do.

Why am I so confident that I have answers you may not? Because in addition to coaching hundreds of clients, I make a point of speaking with HR Directors and CEOs nationwide about the things—large and small—that ultimately disqualify a candidate: from a lack of specificity in their cover letter to an inability to tackle the hard—not to mention the soft—questions, to the seemingly ephemeral ways camaraderie can be destroyed in an interview situation. I've heard it all.

Why do you need this book? Because while you are—as noted above—smart, self-aware, and replete with things to offer, I'm being told things daily that you might not have heard. (For example, these days, interviewers are stopping meetings halfway through and—regardless of whether or not it is true—saying, "I just don't think you're the right fit for us." They're doing it to see if you'll fold or fight. Want to learn how to fight? Read on . . .)

In this world, the ones who get ahead are the ones with the insider information that gives them an edge.

Once you've read this book, this will be you.

I've organized the book into two sections: "Find It" and "Land It."

"Find It" includes everything you need to build the personal, and virtual, presence necessary to make yourself stand out from the thousands of other candidates emailing their resumes to HR in the hope of landing your dream job. It includes information on how to organize your search, write an effective resume, create a professional business card and online presence, and do more than network—network *effectively*.

Once you have the interview booked, you're ready for "Land It." Here, you will discover the research questions you must have the answers to, how to prep for an impromptu interview, strategies for presenting gaps in your resume or skill set, advice on how to manage group/case/social interviews and—now that you're ready to make a deal—tools for managing the all-important compensation conversation.

Your dream job is just around the corner. It's time to go get it.

# WOW

## YOUR WAY INTO THE JOB

## OF YOUR DREAMS

# FIND IT

# JOB SEARCH SECRET: DO IT, DELEGATE IT, OR DELETE IT

Most of us begin our job search methodically, and with purpose. Over time, however, as multiple leads come in, multiple resumes get written, and multiple phone calls are made—both our desk and our email inbox become filled with leads and questions whose neglect paralyzes our thinking and keeps us from moving forward with efficiency. At this point, I recommend instituting the Marine Corps maxim, "Do it, delegate it, or delete it," in order to follow up, and follow through, with greater efficiency.

It's the idea behind touching each piece of paper only once.

Why is this important? Well, not only does it instill confidence in those around you, but it also helps you maintain confidence in yourself. The lurking knowledge that you're procrastinating is a confidence-killer. And in the same way it's hard to feel at the top of your game when you know you've left behind piles of laundry, an unmade bed, and a sink full of dirty dishes, it's hard to go present your best self to the world knowing you have an inbox that's overflowing with requests, complaints, and exhortations.

For example, "Do" items include following through on all leads, from all sources—checking every company's or connection's background. While you may not end up posting resumes or picking up the phone to make a connection on every one, you need to keep the mindset that right now, your job search *is* your job. Don't allow yourself to be sidetracked. What, specifically, are you looking for? Any information on the company's mission/bestselling product/ competition, which can then help you position yourself as being able to contribute to furthering their goals, enhancing their status, or plugging the hole in their offerings via skill sets and ideas that are unique to you.

You might think doing this research is something you can delegate, but I've found this isn't the best use of delegation—a highly underrated skill set, by the way. It's far better to delegate those tasks that many of us use doing our job search as a form of creative procrastination designed as "necessary" work: reformatting our resume, updating our website, even getting our interview wardrobe ready—all of which give you a seemingly morally unimpeachable response to the question "What are you doing to further your search?" when, in fact, they are avoidance behavior. Truly. Unless you are a designer or web developer, these tasks are generally best handed off to those trained in these skill sets. Not only will you give yourself the time you need to focus on what you alone can do, you'll likely end up with a far better looking document or site.

I recommend deleting from your to-do list items along the lines of multiple postings of your resume—and the consequent follow-up—on job search postings websites with "credentials" along the lines of "Lose 9 pounds of belly fat in one day." Focused follow-through on personal recommendations and with accredited sites (say, for example Monster.com or TheLadders.com) is far more likely to yield the results you seek. I also suggest deleting those leads you find via what I call "internet daydreaming." This generally looks like a job that was something you considered doing during your summers off in high school and which just happens to be available in Hawaii.

I do not, however, recommend deleting following up on any personal leads you are offered. While it may be tempting to delete from your to-do list following through on the suggestion you got from your child's camp counselor to get in touch with their cousin "because it seems like you have so much in common," following through could reveal their cousin is the vice president of the firm you've been angling for a connection to for the last six months. (But regardless of whether they result in the outcome you want, you need to remember that personal leads are just that—personal. Thanking the person who offered them is mandatory to building the kind of effective, comprehensive network you will always need.)

As you can see, while it may seem either strident or simplistic, adopting a "Do it, delegate it, or delete it" policy gives you a framework for following up and following through in such a way that your mind is free to give 100% of its focus to your day's priorities.

# NOW YOU'RE SPEAKING MY LANGUAGE

As you begin researching job postings in your area of expertise, it's important to reassure future employers that you are already "speaking their language," as this makes it easier for them to imagine you fitting smoothly into their culture.

If you are a first-time job seeker—or seeking to switch from one industry to another—a great way to do this is to go on a few "informational interviews." These are meetings with higher-ups in your area of interest who can check your resume to ensure you are describing your objective and experience in the language spoken in your desired field. During your interview, they can tell you about trends within the industry that might not be apparent to someone outside the field.

For example, when I first wanted to break into publishing, I went on a few informational interviews, during which I learned that 90% of the people trying to break into that field want to edit fiction—but that a far larger portion of the money made in publishing is made in nonfiction. This enabled me to tweak my resume to highlight the journalistic experience I had had, and to, when I went in for interviews, talk about how I longed to do nothing more than edit books on popular psychology, parenting, how-to. . . .

Once I was speaking the language publishing executives wanted to hear, I was hired to my dream job within a month.

If you are returning to the work force, what you might discover is that—while the basic elements of the job haven't changed—the way people are talking about those elements has.

For example, perhaps you were a consultant working with teams on change management and you used to describe your work as "business process redesign." However, online research reveals that that phrasing has gotten a bad name due to layoffs, and is now referred to as "business transformation." That small update to your resume reassures HR professionals you're up to speed on news in the industry.

Alternatively, perhaps your former job description was, "Managed market research plans" but reading current job postings gives you language such as, "Ran focus groups that uncovered consumer trends—providing sales team with the necessary information for fact-based selling." That's language that's going to make potential employers get in touch.

A great place to check and see how jobs in your desired field are being languaged is TheLadders.com—a site posting jobs paying over $100,000 a year. The employers posting on TheLadders are seeking the most qualified, authoritative candidates imaginable; and they are advertising for them in language that is universally acknowledged within that industry.

Be sure that's the language you are speaking.

# THE ALL-IMPORTANT INFORMATIONAL INTERVIEW

When I was thinking about switching professions, from teaching to publishing, I kept going on interviews and striking out, and I couldn't figure it out. There had to be something I was doing incorrectly, but what was it? To discover, I began going on informational interviews—setting up meetings with people whom I would have loved to have as bosses, but who weren't looking for help. I figured they might be able to tell me how to crack the code. This turned out to be invaluable—this turned out to be how I made the jump.

Here's what happened: when I first tried to break into publishing, I was the ripe old age of twenty-five. I'd been teaching for four years and gotten a Master's Degree. From where I sat, that made me a great candidate. From where a future boss sat, that made me a liability. I discovered their concern was that no sooner would they get me trained to their liking than I would move on. Knowing this, I was able to go into an actual interview and say, "I understand that my age and experience might be a concern—that you feel I might leave in a few months. I understand and can tell you that I'm willing to make an eighteen month commitment to this job once you offer it to me."

Bingo.

The purpose of an informational interview is to find out both what companies in your field are looking for and—just as importantly—what they are not. Also, to discover what their concerns might be from looking at you, and your resume.

Additionally, informational interviews are a great place to find out what *not* to say as well as what you should say—because over the years I have found that in every industry there is one question you can ask, or statement you can make, that just drives people *wild*.

For example, when I worked in publishing that phrase was, "And I know my book would be great on *Oprah*."

Aaaaauugh. I mean, their book might very well be great on *Oprah*—but getting your book on *Oprah* is a bit like getting struck by lightning. The effect of a prospective author saying this was only to make everyone in the room think, "High maintenance. Back away slowly."

The fact that the interview is informational doesn't mean you don't have to prep just as carefully as you would if there were a job at stake. You should know your interviewer's resume inside and out. You should have a list of questions you'd like to have answered: are there any skills I should fine-tune? Are there any immediate red flags you see when you look at my resume? Are there any new trends in the industry I should be aware of? As noted above, is there anything I should absolutely never, ever say?

Now it might seem that people in these positions don't have the time or energy to give to these interviews. I rarely found this to be true. The people I know who've been shut down had often opened with, "Let me take you to lunch." While this is a lovely offer, these people are busy. They don't want to commit to lunch. So, set yourself up for success by respecting their time limits up front, ask them, "May I come in to speak with you for fifteen minutes at the beginning or end of your day?"

Two other great benefits of this kind of interviewing are that once you get an interview with someone in their field, you can often call back and ask if there's anything in particular about that person that would be important for you to know. Also, if they were sufficiently impressed with you, they will have you in mind when someone in their field is looking to hire a new person for their team.

Informational interviews are a win/win/win—and all those wins are for you. You get the experience of interviewing, you get the information, and you get the future connection.

# MASTER THE MEDIUM

While it's a bit surprising to me that this needs to be put in writing, experience has shown me that there are a number of elements that need to be addressed regarding email addresses.

I'll begin with the most glaring infraction I see—generally among younger job seekers—which is the use of addresses along the lines of hotkitty@gmail.com, yogichick@aol.com, shaft@hotmail.com . . . These are not appropriate email addresses for use in any situation.

"But," I've had people protest, "I just use these with my friends! I would never use them when I'm looking for a job." OK. I believe that you would never consciously choose to use this address during your job search. That said, we all know there are days when we aren't at the top of our game, for whatever reason: you're sleep deprived, you're checking multiple accounts on your tiny, but indispensable, PDA, you leave your phone on the table and your friend finds it "funny" to forward last night's exploits to all your recent contacts, and suddenly the email's out there and you're cleaning up an interpersonal gaffe that simply didn't have to happen.

Given this, I recommend closing down any accounts you may have with suggestive, cute, silly, personal monikers. While I'm certain this makes me sound like the world's worst killjoy, that's a title I'm willing to own. (Though I would not, of course, set myself up as killjoy@yahoo.com.)

Additionally, I'm not a fan of obscure combinations of letters and numbers. While it might be immediately apparent, and a helpful aide-mémoire for you, that your address is your initials and your birthday or the date Beyoncé rocked the Super Bowl or some such, you are making others work too hard to remember it.

And when you make me work too hard I feel stupid, and when I feel stupid, I don't like you.

What then, do I recommend you do? My suggestion for

job seekers of any age is to buy your name as a dot.com For example, I own FrancesJones.com, FrancesCJones.com, FrancesColeJones.com, plus the myriad addresses used for my books and my business. Why? Because linking your email to a service that is used by millions of others (Gmail, AOL, Yahoo, etc.) doesn't leave the impression of you as unique—as a force to be reckoned with. Buying your name tells others you take yourself seriously, and they need to, too. With this in hand—should your name be John Doe—you can set yourself up as John@JohnDoe.com. This can be done at Register.com, NetworkSolutions.com, and Active-Domain.com or—my favorite—pairNIC.com. Their customer service is outstanding.

And, while we're on the subject of formality and informality on the World Wide Web, I am going to request you clean up your Facebook/Twitter, etc., pages. Because although I have no doubt your trip to Vegas with your friends was memorable (or memorable now that you've posted the pictures online), these should not be available for the world to see—and thinking the world isn't going to look is, in this day and age, laughable. As many of you know who read publications from *The Wall Street Journal* to the *New York Post,* job candidates across any number of industries—from bankers to police officers—have been weeded out due to inappropriate postings on their personal pages. Also consider that the latest vetting form for the White House requires candidates to list "all aliases or 'handles' you have used to communicate on the Internet," everything they've written, "including, but not limited to, any posts or comments on blogs or other websites," links to their Facebook or MySpace pages and any potentially embarrassing "electronic communication, including but not limited to an email, text message or instant message." But it's not just White House jobs—in fact, in addition to checking your pages on their own time, recently, I've heard stories of potential employers asking you to open your Facebook page mid-interview. . . .

I sincerely hope that gave you pause.

How am I classifying inappropriate? Any postings referencing the intimate details of your personal relationship, your GI tract, or your mental health; and any photos in which you are drinking, smoking, leering, sneering, suggestively posed, or otherwise indisposed. If you are in doubt, I recommend asking yourself the following question: "Does this entry/picture make me sound/look like I can be trusted with $100,000?" If it doesn't, get rid of it. These portals are your public face—or shop window—to the world. You wouldn't want to run into the HR Director with whom you just interviewed scantily clad, slightly inebriated, or making lewd gestures with your friends on the street, don't let him or her find you that way on your home page.

# THE POLISHED (HOME) PROFESSIONAL

Whether you are freelancing as you look for a job, or have made looking for a job your fulltime job, it is critical that you always appear professional. With this in mind, here are a few tips for ensuring you always present your best self (and a few tips for improving efficiency):

1. If you don't already know, learn how to make address labels on your home printer—hand-addressed mail looks less official.

2. When you are sending something via snail mail, be sure the stamp you have chosen is appropriate—e.g., don't send something with a "Season's Greetings" stamp in August, or a "Love" stamp just because the Post Office is pushing them around Valentine's Day.

3. Consider a separate phone line, especially if you have kids. If this is not possible, please make sure your greeting presents your best self. Your name should be clearly stated; any alternate number offered shouldn't be given so quickly your caller has to call back three times to write it down; and there should be no background noise.

4. You can easily "expand" the size of your office by incorporating the Post-It Table Top Pad: these white board–sized Post-Its are a great way to give a conference room–sized feel to a closet-sized space.

5. A "countdown clock" is a great way to ensure you stay on task. Used for planning everything from weddings to conferences, numerous models are available at Alibaba.com.

# HAVE A SCHEME (OR AT LEAST A BLOG)

Even a few years ago, having a personal presence online was seen as, at best, a luxury or at worst an eccentricity. These days, it's essential. If you can't be Googled, you don't exist. Given this it's critical for you to have a blog or personal website of your own; not doing so signals to employers that you are out of touch with modern rhythms.

So, let's start with blogs. Before we go any further, we'd better agree on what a blog is: a blog is a web-based commentary site, usually written in a first person, conversational manner about just about anything that you can imagine, and displayed in reverse chronological order. It can (and I recommend it should) include text, pictures, and links to videos, news items, etc., that interest, annoy, or inspire you. Done well, they offer an incredibly effective yet low-cost way to establish a basic web presence, to build up your personal brand visibility, and to enhance your credibility. If you run your own business, they're a great way to influence the public "conversation" about your company, gain customer insight, and communicate with the other stakeholders in your business (employees, suppliers, etc.).

How do you get started on a blog? There are a number of free sites to get you started, like WordPress.com, Blogger.com, or home.spaces.live.com. Wiki Blog even has a free eight-part video entitled "How to Start a Blog" available at wikiHow.com/Start-a-Blog.

These sites or others you can find will walk you through the nuts and bolts of the process. Here are my thoughts on tone and content:

- Use your own voice—don't write as if there is someone over your shoulder: authenticity is essential.
- While you should be honest and open, you should also be respectful of your subject and your audi-

ences: no insults, no profanity. Keep criticism to a minimum.

- Link to those who interest or influence you; the more you reference, and have links to on your blog, the stronger your presence will be within the blogosphere.

- If you're blogging specifically about your business, don't treat blogging like advertising—it's a conversation, not a sermon. For that reason, make sure that you listen and respond to the feedback that you receive.

- Having your name, your product/company's name in the URL generally means Google will index it higher with respect to rank.

- Once you begin it, it's important to keep it fairly current. I'm not saying you have to update it daily— or even weekly. But I wouldn't let more than two to three weeks go by without saying something.

- What keeps people coming back to your blog? Content they can use. The more your blog includes essential/inside information and/or quirky/funny anecdotes they can't get elsewhere the more likely they are to return.

Once you have your blog established, link it to your LinkedIn, Facebook, Twitter, etc. profiles. They all have spaces where URLs can be added to your personal information.

The bigger step is, of course, establishing your own site. This can either be personal, or for your business.

How to begin? The first thing to know is that a personal site isn't just a giant blog: you'll need a scheme. Whether you decide to build the site yourself (sites such as Register.com, NetworkSolutions.com, and Active-Domain.com have templates on-hand for this) or have someone build it for you, (take a look at B2kcorp.com), I recommend starting by writing a schemata: a detailed document that includes every element you want the site to include. As you put this together, it's important to look both at the competition to make sure there's nothing you're neglecting that appears to be mandatory elsewhere, and at the sites you frequent that may seem on the surface to have nothing to do with your field, but have features you find compelling, and then asking yourself, "How can I make that work for me?" I would also have you think ahead to what you might not need at the moment, but will want to have later, such as video, so you are sure you begin to design something that has the capacity to build out those elements one day.

What elements do I think every site should include? In my experience, personal sites should include:

- Your bio (This is not a resume, but a paragraph or two filled with active language that lays out specific details about what you've accomplished, and why others should care.)
- A professional headshot (While I know these can be expensive, they are well worth the money. In my dream world, they're not only professional-looking, they convey your personality, too—there's nothing wrong with smiling. I don't recommend having your arms crossed over your chest, or leaning your chin on your hand, both of which "read" as discomfort.)
- A statement of your goals
- Your contact details
- Links to sites you frequent (Again, the more you include, the better. If these can show a breadth of interests to demonstrate general curiosity, then you really make my heart sing.)

If available, you might also include a portfolio of papers and/or PowerPoint presentations that you've written or executed, photos and/or video of you presenting at conferences, and—perhaps—one or two general interests. (If you do choose to include these, I will tell you that one of my clients who works in the banking industry told me that they do look to see if you've played team sports.) If you do post samples of your work, make sure you assert copyright by adding a "©," your name or organization, and the year.

With regard to design and upkeep, you want to think of your website as your shop window to the world. As with bricks-and-mortar stores, it's worth investing significant time and resources to ensure it's welcoming, easy to navigate, and provides readers with the essentials. If you can find a way to offer a free "gift with purchase" for coming by, such as expertise, a quote, inside information—an actual free gift!—so much the better, as, again, this will keep them coming back for more. If you have someone in-house who's up to putting together a newsletter that provides readers with valuable industry information/advice/tips, this is a great way to build your customer mailing list. At minimum, it is absolutely vital that if you offer an email for information or service, you or someone else respond to any queries received in a timely way. This can't be an email box that you check once a month.

To my mind, the best stores are the ones that catch your eye going by, you enter with expectation, and you leave saying, "I didn't even know I needed this—now I don't know how I lived without it!" With the proper planning, creativity, and upkeep, your blog or website will be the same.

# BUSINESS CARD BLUNDERS

Despite the fact that it's now preposterously easy to find one another online, both newly minted professionals and more experienced job seekers must have a business card to exchange.

Do I have specific suggestions with regard to other elements of your business card? Not surprisingly, I do. And while there are as many permutations of business cards as there are businesses—and there are no hard and fast rules about what is "acceptable" and what isn't—I'd like to include the following list of recommendations:

- As noted, have them. Even if you are currently employed, you should not be using your firm's business cards for networking. If you are not employed, you should still have business cards that state your full name and complete contact information.
- Include multiple ways to reach you: land line, cell, Skype number, email, snail mail address; you don't want it to look cluttered, but you do want to give people confidence you can be reached—and reassure them that you're in step with modern technology.
- If you aren't employed by a firm, and so the holder of a particular title, I'd prefer that you not include a description of what you do, because while you may indeed be a writer, editor, agent, or producer, there's a whiff of desperation to including that on your card.
- I don't recommend including slogans, mission statements, affirmations, inspirational sayings, etc.
- I prefer you not include any design elements on offer at your local printing shop. You're unique. Your card should be, too.
- That said, unless it's your profession, I'd proceed with caution with regard to creating a design element of your own. Given the number

of variables in play—scale, color, typeface—it's far better to have your personal "brand identity" professionally created.

- I'm not a fan of unusual trim sizes. A slightly larger or square card may be difficult for others to fit into their wallets. Slightly smaller can come across as precious.
- Don't skimp on your paper quality. Yes, it's an additional expense to have cards printed on heavy stock, but it makes them far more memorable (and durable) for the receiver.

Why do these dos and don'ts matter so much? Because ultimately your card is selling you, and you need something whose information and quality of design and printing are a direct reflection of the value you offer.

If you find yourself in a situation where you've forgotten your card, rather than scrawling your information on the back of a napkin or piece of scrap paper, I would ask if they have a spare and then write your information on the back of that—we often throw out old scraps of paper when cleaning our wallets, but we're unlikely to throw out our own business cards, so there's less of a possibility your details will land in the trash.

In Japan, the custom when handing others your card is to hold it with two hands and bow when it's offered. While I don't think it's necessary to go to that extreme, I also don't want a hand-off that looks like you're doing a drug deal (something I see a lot): one which includes furtive glances at the surrounding people on the part of the giver and studied nonchalance on the part of the receiver. When you take another's card—regardless of the value you perceive they offer—you need to treat it as valuable. Make a point of putting it into your wallet, or purse. Thrusting it into the pocket of your suit can leave the giver thinking they're more likely to get a call from your drycleaner than they are to get a call from you.

# THE ART OF THE RESUME

For many people, sitting down to write their resume is a gruesome and grueling experience. I get it. It can be difficult to encapsulate the breadth and depth of what you have to offer on one sheet of paper. Alternatively, there are also moments when what you have seems shockingly sparse.

Luckily there are ways around both of these conundrums.

## The Chronological Resume

If you are fairly new to job hunting, I recommend putting together a chronological resume, listing any jobs, internships, etc., you might have had starting from the present and working backward.

I am not a fan of listing an "Objective" at the head of your resume. It seems redundant—of course your objective is to be hired into that industry/position. Why else would you be applying for the job?

As you describe the work you did in each position, be sure to be specific. It's not enough to say, "Oversaw the creation of marketing materials." You need to say, "Researched and created marketing materials used in presentations by both the CEO and COO."

If you have won awards, or received other forms of recognition, include that as a section entitled "Awards and Recognition." Note, please, that holding the title of "Beer-Pong Pasha" is unlikely to help you get your foot in the door.

If you have unique skills, list them under additional skills. Please note: a) that they need to be unique not just within your circle of friends, but within the context of the thousands of candidates who are likely applying for the same position; and b) they need to be applicable to the job in question. It's super that you won the national hacky sack competition, but it won't get you far in investment banking.

Speaking of banking: those investment-industry types are often excited about candidates who have participated in team sports. If you have done so, include that information under "Sports History."

## The Skills-Based Resume

If you have a patchy work history or are returning to work after a break; if you're changing careers and want to emphasize transferable skills; if you don't want to look like a job hopper; or if you're applying for a job that requires skills you haven't used in a while, I recommend putting together a skills-based resume. These resumes group your work under headings such as "Marketing," "Team Building," "Strategy," etc.—all of which can appear under the heading, "Overview of Experience." (That said, if you use one, be ready to give a clear job chronology in interviews.)

Within each category I would then list the times and positions in which you used the skill in question. I would also be sure to state the outcome of that work. So, instead of "Oversaw the creation of marketing materials," you would state, "Oversaw the creation of marketing materials used by a sales force of 50+, leading to a subsequent rise in the bottom line from X to Y."

*A Note on Naming*

Once you have created this marvelous document, please do not name it Resume.doc. While this may work beautifully for you—given that you are likely to have only one resume in your system—it is utterly maddening to the HR professionals who receive hundreds of resumes a day; and who then have to take the time to rename them and delete the original. In all frankness, this is usually when they delete your file entirely. With this in mind, my suggestion would be to name your resume "Your Name.Resume.Month Year.doc." So, for example, mine would be "Frances Jones.Resume.September 20XX."

Regardless of what kind of resume you put together, you need to tweak it almost every time you send it out to ensure that the skills required for the position in question have been highlighted.

*Look for Angels Wearing Overalls*

As Thomas Edison told us, "The reason that so few people recognize opportunity is that it comes dressed in overalls and looks a lot like hard work." This idea is vital to the networking you do during your job search, when making one more phone call, having one more coffee, or going on one more informational interview can seem like you're simply wasting your time or spinning your wheels—not to mention, not jibing with where you feel you should be in your career.

That said, I can state unequivocally that some of the most extraordinary clients I've worked with have been the result of connections I made while having breakfast with a friend's aunt, attending a client's son's 8th grade graduation, or tossing around small talk with the cashier at the local health food store.

To be clear, connecting in this way is not about ingratiating yourselves to others in a nauseating way, nor is it about employing the slick negotiating methods of a snake oil salesman. Not at all; in fact, it is the exact opposite. Rather, it stems from having an unwavering intention to contribute positively to any situation, and employing the following three basic facts of personal presentation:

1.  Every interaction you have with another person is a presentation of yourself;

2.  How you present yourself in these situations directly impacts the results you receive, both in the moment and going forward; and

3.  Life is business, and business is life; they are one and the same. In other words, you are *always* networking whether you think you are or not—

and the best networking not only leaves the people you meet feeling good about the encounter, it leaves you feeling good about yourself.

But, you're asking, is it really that important to wow the barista at my local Starbucks the way I try to wow my future boss?

In a word, yes. The dividends you're paid by investing the best you have in any and every situation pay off in immediate, long term, and often as-yet-unforeseen results. The long-term effect of showing up every day, in every interaction, as your best possible self requires the constant honing of your organizational, networking, and communication skills—skills that, as they become increasingly more refined, perform like compound interest, earning you far more than you ever believed was possible.

Here's an example: I recently picked up some of my most lucrative, ongoing work from making myself available for an initial small, somewhat absurd, request: talking to an A-list celebrity in the Ladies' room for fifteen minutes about what she planned to say during her star turn at a major midtown Manhattan Christmas event.

Being able to think on my feet in that situation earned me her endless gratitude—gratitude that has morphed into ongoing work that will see me through the coming year.

For this reason, I strongly recommend approaching every encounter as an unopened gift, and accepting any and every networking invitation regardless of how useless or uninviting the prospect might be. After all, standing in line for coffee while listening to music and texting your BFF, or planning your evenings around the latest install-ment of your favorite HBO drama, is not exactly putting yourself in the path of serendipity.

Speaking of activities that initially don't seem worth your time, I have also found that some of the most valuable experi-ence I've gained has come from doing jobs and learning skills that initially didn't seem worth an investment of effort. For example, when I was looking for a job as an editor in pub-lishing, I made a point of taking both copyediting and proof-reading classes, despite the fact that neither of these skills is integral to an editor's job. Why, then, was this information useful? Well, in addition to impressing interviewers with my commitment to the industry, it gave me instant credibility with the copyeditors and proofreaders with whom I worked once I got the job—I understood their language, constraints, and needs, which meant when I needed a favor, like extra time with a manuscript, extra patience with an author, they were more likely to accede. All of which improved my standing with those at the top.

How, then, can you begin to recognize when the knock at

the door is, in fact, opportunity? One way is to broaden your definition of the job you are seeking—to examine your knee jerk reaction that thus-and-such is beneath you. For example, are there skill sets within your industry that others have but you haven't acquired? Steps in the chain of product production you don't have a grasp on? Internal communication processes you haven't bothered to examine, much less master? Getting in the trenches with regard to this knowledge will not only make you more effective in your next interview, but it will make you a more effective leader once you have the job in-hand: the people working for you will know that not only can you talk the talk, you can walk the walk. Two of my most successful—and well-liked—CEOs are so effective because they took the time to understand the ins and outs of their rank-and-file employees' days. One, a retail magnate, set himself to work folding sweaters at a major department store during the holiday rush; the other, the CEO of a food services giant, learned how to drive the eighteen wheelers his team was using to transport products coast to coast. Not only did both find their experiences helpful to their understanding of their companies, they found them invaluable for building credibility and morale.

As Samuel Goldwyn said, "I find that the harder I work, the more luck I seem to have." I'm guessing the same will be true for you.

# NAME DROP WITH DISCRETION

One of the more common missteps I see at networking events is a tendency to establish credibility by letting others know whom you know, rather than what you do. This name-dropping often sounds like, "So, you design handbags?" "Yes—you may have seen X celebrity carrying it in the recent issue of *People*. She's such a good friend." Or, "So, you're a writer?" "I am. X, Y, and Z have all endorsed my books. We've known each other for years."

The trouble with this follow-up is that you've now

moved the conversation away from how your business/
product/service might improve the life of the person you're
speaking with; instead, they're in a conversation about your
Rolodex—a topic they're unlikely to find as interesting.

How can you establish your credibility without putting
others off—particularly if you do have significant connections? My suggestion would be to find a way to link the life
of the person in question to the connection you know—so
you might say, "Yes, I design handbags that are particularly
popular with working mothers, as they have the capacity
for both computers and kid paraphernalia. Do you have
kids?" From there, it's easy enough to work in your well-
known chum who's also a working mom.

In addition to overt name-dropping, I also caution my
clients about having too many "best friends," as there's something equally disquieting about meeting someone who—
no matter who you mention—responds by announcing
they've been best friends with that person since they met
in the paddling pool. My request is that you concentrate
instead on making the person with whom you're speaking
feel like they are the most important person in your life.

All of that said, are there times when it's useful to do
some name-dropping? Occasionally, yes. There are people
who are reassured by knowing that you've had the experience of working for a name-brand firm; that you attended a

Big Ten school; that you count the local celebrity as a close friend. In every case, however, you will appear much cooler if you "bury the lead" when talking about it—if you spend a bit of time asking the person you're speaking with about him or herself first. There's simply never any need for a sentence along the lines of "Last summer after I left Harvard, my BFF Ben Affleck and I were inseparable until I began my job at Goldman Sachs."

Because all they are thinking at that point is, "Stop the bombing."

# DO GO THERE

The phrase "Don't go there" has entered common usage, and become the shorthand way of telling people to abandon their current line of reasoning or questioning. I'm here to tell you that, more often than not, you should go there—in this case the "there" in question being the decision-maker in charge of your inquiry, your request, or your future.

Let me give you an example: a few years ago, my brother (with whom I often do some consulting, although he lives in Italy) and I were being considered for a large consulting job in Manhattan. I had met with the potential client once and knew we were among the final three candidates being considered. As the process was drawing to a close, I said, "Oh, and Milo will be here next week if you'd like to meet him, too." They said yes. I bought my brother a plane ticket. He flew in. We got the job.

His "going there" (or in this case, "coming here") made all the difference.

What might this look like for you?

Well, for example, say you find a posting for your dream job on the web. While it's important to post your resume and information according to the guidelines presented I would also recommend writing a note to the CEO/CFO/VP to whom you would ultimately report noting that you've done so, but also including the specifics of the value you plan to add to the company on your arrival, then dropping that note in the mail, or at the office itself. Please note, however, that this just means dropping the note at the office. This does not mean attempting to get past the gatekeepers to plead your case. (I can't emphasize enough how important this: leaping out of the woodwork at people is incredibly off-putting.)

That said—as noted—physically putting yourself in the person's sightline can be a great thing to do, provided it's accomplished with finesse. Always remember, attempting to outwit callers like you is likely one of the many reasons the gatekeeper got their job. Given that, it's critically important for you to work on establishing camaraderie with them by introducing yourself, finding out their name, and asking their advice about the best way to move forward. The key word there is advice. When they feel like you're attempting to circumnavigate them, they will block you on principle; when you defer to their experience/expertise and enlist their aid by giving them the "because" behind why you are making your request, they are much more likely to accede. (As was discussed in *How to Wow*, giving people the "because" behind why a request is being made increases the possibility of their cooperation from 60 to 94%.)

When you do ask their advice, I would put it in both the most proactive, and the most low-stakes, way imaginable: "I'm planning to be in your neighborhood/in town next week. Do you think there is five minutes at either the beginning or the end of any day that he would be able to see me? I ask because . . ." Tacking it onto another trip you are ostensibly making to the area keeps you from seeming too much like a stalker. Putting a five-minute time limit on it demonstrates that you recognize this is an imposition. As noted, the "because" helps them feel they are part of the decision-making process.

Should you be rebuffed, you want to take it with good humor, "Of course. I just thought I'd suggest it. I'm in and out of your part of town quite a bit, though, so I may give you a call again in a week or so." When you do call back, remember, it's a fresh start: yes, you know the gatekeeper's name, but what's been going on in their world? Find out. They have a rich and full life outside your phone calls. Making the time to get to know something about that helps strengthen your connection. Then explain you're again going to be in their neighborhood, give them the "because" behind why you'd like five minutes with their boss, and ask for a specific five minutes of his or her time. Whether it's granted this time or not, I'd suggest writing the gatekeeper a thank you note for their trouble. Because if they're still keeping you at bay, this is just the kind of personal touch that might have them put in a favorable word for you, which means the next call could be their boss looking for you.

# LAND IT

# GETTING A JOB IS YOUR JOB

As noted, many of us begin our job search with a certain degree of focus and determination. As a certain amount of days, weeks, and even months go by, however, we find ourselves losing steam. It becomes easy to fill up an entire day changing the fonts on our resume, or searching the internet for "dream jobs" that look a lot like we've entered the witness protection program.

The thing is, right now, looking for a job is your job. Sleeping in until 10 a.m., checking Facebook, meeting a friend for lunch at your local coffee shop, then doing a little light internet surfing is not searching for a job. You will have far greater mental—and material—success if you set your alarm, shower, shave, walk around the block, and get to your desk by 9 a.m.

In my world, "Look good. Feel good" always applies, but never more than during a job search.

Speaking of how you look and feel: as many of you know, when your body is in distress, it shuts down all nonessential functions. (This is why fear so often causes our mouths to go dry: salivation is, essentially, non-essential.)

This is because our bodies are infinitely wise.

If you are having trouble focusing on your job search, my recommendation would be to apply this same, innate wisdom to the process: take a long, hard look at what activities you currently consider essential and then consider whether or not they are, in fact, so. (I mean, I'm guessing up until a few seconds ago you thought salivation was essential, too, and *that's* on the list. . . . You really don't have *anything* that can go?) Ask yourself: is it really necessary for me to have that lunch, or do I just feel like getting caught up with so-and-so? Do I really need to redesign my website *completely* before I send out my resume, or is it sharp enough to focus instead on getting something posted today? Do I really have to have my five-year plan complete before I go pitch my idea, or can I start making calls next week?

In short, are some of the excuses just the job search version of, "I can't go to the gym until I lose five pounds"?

So, get in there. Punch the clock. Put in the time. The focus you fine-tune today will stand you in good stead when your boss turns to you and says, "I was hoping you could put in a few late nights this week. OK?"

# RESEARCH ROUNDUP

I've talked a lot about doing your background research on the company, and many of you may be thinking, "Well, that sounds great in theory, but what specifically am I looking for, and where exactly am I supposed to look for it?

Begin by taking an in-depth look at the website of the company with whom you're interviewing. It is not enough to simply glance through the home page and look up the bio of the person with whom you're interviewing. You need to have a grasp on their history, their mission statement, their corporate structure, their C-level executive team. . . . At this time I would also do a search on who their competition is and why.

All of this will stand you in good stead as you begin to craft the answers to the following nine questions:

1. Why you want to work in the industry.
   This is an often-overlooked softball question. For example, if you're talking to Citibank, it's possible they will begin with, "Why do you want to be in finance?" A question that almost demands a story along the lines of, "From the time I was X years old . . ." includes a precipitating incident, and concludes with, "and I've been passionate about it ever since." This answer is particularly important if you are changing sectors (i.e., moving from garden design to retail fashion). You must have a reason beyond "I need a job"—even if that's true.

2. Why you want to work for that particular company.
   Here is where you speak to their mission, their corporate values, their vision, etc., and then position yourself as being able to contribute to furthering their goals, enhancing their status, or plugging the hole in their offerings via skill sets

and ideas that are unique to you—how do their goals mesh with yours? As in a good cover letter, this is a chance to speak about *their* needs in terms of *your* abilities. (Cover letter side note: the basic opening theme of cover letters should be "My understanding is that your company needs X, Y, and Z," i.e., open with what you know about THEM and what you believe are their needs. You can *then* move on to why you can meet those needs, "especially because this has been a lifelong goal," etc. . . . The point is, you want to open by talking about them and their requirements, and then show how well you match. Do this, and they'll be pleasantly surprised.)

3. What their best selling product is and why.

   If it's a consumer product, you need to have tried it (if you haven't.) Additionally, make sure that you're not wearing, carrying, driving, etc., the competition. One consultant that I know who worked in the telecoms industry was smart enough to keep three brands of cell-phones in his briefcase. Before meetings, he would move SIM cards from phone to phone as appropriate. He started this practice ever since potential clients at Palm commented on the Blackberry he was carrying. One MBA student that I know borrowed a friend's Ford to attend his interview there—when he got the job, he sold his Toyota before reporting for work!

4. In this vein, know who their competition is, and why.

   If they are not a consumer brand, or you are new to the industry and aren't quite sure, Hoover's (Hoovers.com) is a big help for this, as are stock reports on the company or industry which can be found from brokerages like Charles Schwab (CharlesSchwab.com). What I've discovered is that even if the company I am interested is not publicly traded, the broker will have reports that explain in laymen's terms the big players in an industry, how the companies in it have been doing lately, all the latest important news about the business, etc. And unlike looking at whatever Google throws up that day, you can also be sure that this industry information has been sorted and sifted for relevance and (relative) even-handedness.

5. How many employees/offices they have (and the locations of those offices).

6. Do they have any subsidiary brands.

7. Have they been in the news for industry infighting.

This last one can be tough and so, is often overlooked even by the best of us (remember when Tiger Woods thanked Arthur Andersen—as opposed to Andersen Consulting—for sponsoring a golf tournament when he was on Andersen Consulting's payroll; the partners were in the audience, and the two were in the midst of a bitter corporate divorce). That said, they don't call it the World Wide Web for nothing—do take the time to check beyond the first five entries Google throws up. (If nothing turns up by entry twenty, you've likely done your due diligence, however.)

8. As much knowledge as possible on your interviewer's background.

While you don't want to walk in with a creepy level of detail, you should know where he or she went to school, how long they've been with the company, etc. Questions about their experience with the company—what do they like best about the corporate culture, etc.—are also a nice thing to ask should they inquire, "Do you have any questions for me?" ("Do you have any questions for me?" is also a good time to ask about their company's plans for growth over the next five years.)

9. The general salary range for that position within the industry.

   You won't want to bring up a number unless they do—but should they ask what your proposed salary might be, you want to be able to give them a range that's in the industry ballpark. (This is definitely not the time to say, "I don't know . . . what are you offering?" The best way to find this is to look up similar jobs being advertised on sites such as Monster.com, TheLadders.com, etc.

Should you need information on an industry about which you're not terribly knowledgeable, I recommend you go immediately to HarvardBusiness.org, home of Harvard Business School case studies. Covering disciplines from accounting to entrepreneurship, finance to marketing, negotiations to competitive strategy—and available for less than ten dollars apiece— these bits of "potted knowledge" offer you the ability to speak with a far greater degree of authority. Designed to tell MBA's everything they need to know about the corporate drivers of a company or industry so they can offer intelligent analyses about the case in question, they guarantee instant confidence.

# BE "DRESS READY"

Often, we are so concerned with preparing for what we will say in the interview, that we don't spend an adequate amount of time considering what we will be wearing. While there aren't a lot of hard and fast rules (OK . . . there are a few; I'll pass them along) there are a few things that I always want you to keep in mind.

What's not negotiable?

Don't break the "Too Rule": not too much leg, not too much cleavage, not too much chest hair, not too much perfume/cologne. It's an interview, not a date.

Speaking of things I never want to see: visible bra straps. I don't care if it's "underwear meant as outerwear." It's not acceptable. In that vein, no see-through blouses or camisoles under blazers.

Don't wear heels that are so high that your interviewer leaves you in the dust as he or she strides through the office. Again, this is not a date.

OK, now that that is out of the way, what do I recommend?

Researching the company online should have given you an idea of the corporate culture and subsequent dress code. While banking and the law will likely forever necessitate a navy suit and sober tie, there is a bit more play in some of the creative professions; i.e., you might be able to wear a more exciting tie.

Yes, I always recommend a tie. It's better to be slightly overdressed than slightly underdressed. If you get to the interview and everyone is running around in cutoffs and flip flops you can take it off and put it in your pocket, but have it on hand.

Ladies, I am a big fan of a dress; but if you'd like to wear a suit with a skirt that's entirely up to you. Since some people view wearing pants as anathema I'd sport the skirt rather than a trouser suit until you get the job.

Blue is the color we trust the most (and it photographs

best) so I recommend a blue shirt. Within the spectrum of possible shades of blue, you want a cornflower, or French blue.

Shine your shoes. Shine your briefcase.

Speaking of shiny shoes: The Marine Corps recommends keeping a 'dress-ready' uniform in their kit at all times in case a general suddenly arrives on base. I recommend you have an interview-ready outfit in your closet at all times, plus up-to-the-minute business cards, resume, and/or portfolio. This means you can spend the time in between the phone call and your interview refreshing your mind on the details of the company in question, not running to the drycleaner or copy shop.

)

# JUST SAY YES

Every now and then an unexpected phone call is good news: in this case, you're asked to come in for an impromptu interview. In these moments, it's possible you might not be in a job hunting frame of mind, and so your answer to, "Can you come in today at 3?" might sound something like, "Hang on. I need to check with my babysitter/my partner/ my trainer." . . . This is not good. In these moments, the only answer to the question is, "Yes." After that, hang up and figure out the details on your own time. Similarly, if inquiries are made about a skill set that can be acquired via a weekend's worth of hard work on your part—for example, "Do you know how to run a focus group? Coordinate a marketing newsletter e-blast? Embed a video in a Keynote presentation?" Even if in the moment you have *no idea* how you might do such a thing, your answer should run along the following lines:

> INTERVIEWER: So, do you know how to embed a video in a PowerPoint presentation?
>
> YOU: *(Internal dialogue)* What?? Is that even possible?? *(External dialogue)* "That isn't something that's required at my job—which has been an ongoing frustration for me since it's a valuable skill to have. What I've done to address that is research it on my own time. If you feel it's critical for me to know, I'll have it mastered by my start date."

# JOB INTERVIEW TIMELINE

Once you've got the job interview, it can suddenly feel like there are any number of things you need to tackle immediately. In order to help my clients prioritize—and keep from becoming overwhelmed—I put together the following job interview timeline:

*72 hours before*

- Start your research. As noted, this is something you need to do yourself.

- Decide on what you will be wearing and take anything that needs to be cleaned to the drycleaner.

## 48 hours before

- Put together your list of potential questions and answers and practice out loud. If at all possible, have someone you trust videotape your Q&A, watch it with you, and offer constructive feedback.
- I've said it before, but it bears repeating: make sure that you have a work-relevant, crisp response to that hardball interview question, "So, tell me about yourself . . ."

## 24 hours before

- Pick up the dry cleaning you took in two days ago.
- Check the weather report and make any necessary changes or additions to your wardrobe depending on what you discover: umbrella, different shoes or jacket, etc.
- MapQuest your route or program your GPS; it's not enough to have a general idea of where you're headed.

- Know where you are planning to park, and how long it will take to get from there to your interview. Many big companies have multiple entrances. HR departments are pretty good about specifying these, but be sure you know the one to which your headed. On some corporate "campuses" there is even an internal shuttle bus for you to catch once you are on their grounds. (I have seen this at both software companies and pharmaceutical companies). Again, HR is usually pretty good about preparing you for this, but it's important to be mentally prepared.

- Print out two copies of your resume: one for you and one for your interviewer. I can't tell you how often I've heard stories of interviewers not having a client's resume in front of them. Having two gives you the opportunity to help them look better when they're shuffling through the papers on their desk saying, "I know I had it right here . . ." (That said, don't make a big deal of handing it over. An easy, "Oh, I brought an extra," is perfect.)

- Polish your shoes. If you have "Edge Dressing" or "Scuff Cover"—two truly miraculous shoe-maintenance products—be sure to detail the edges. This is what the professionals do.

- Polish your briefcase or portfolio and make sure it's loaded with a pad, the aforementioned two resumes, and two pens. One big caution: buff these carefully when you're finished—the last thing you need is black polish from your lovely-looking portfolio ending up on your slightly sweating palms, freshly laundered shirt or trousers, etc.
- If you're a smoker, you might consider getting a nicotine patch (not gum) to help with your nerves that day.

### Day of

- Don't brush your teeth in your interview outfit. (Do brush them, however.) The last thing you need is a big blob of toothpaste, or a water stain, on your freshly ironed shirt.
- Double check that you have picture ID with you in case you have to identify yourself to security.

### 15 minutes before

- Be outside the building. If you do want or need something to eat or drink, please don't choose something that might stain (coffee, tea, etc.) or explode. (Yes, I saw that happen with a jelly doughnut.)

## 10 minutes before

- Be in the lobby. This will give you time to clear security if necessary; wander into the wrong elevator bank and correct your course, stop on multiple floors if you happen to be coming in at the beginning or middle of the day, etc.

- If there is a parking ticket to validate, get this done now. You don't want to have to come back in sheepishly after a triumphant exit. In any case, never ask the executive or the HR people to do this for you if you can avoid it.

## 5 minutes before

- Be in front of the receptionist. Please be sure to greet this person courteously both on your way in, and on your way out, of the building. Remember, he or she will likely be polled as to what they thought of you.

# INTERVIEW FORMATS

When most of us think of interviewing, we think about a one-on-one sit-down. While this is the most common scenario, I want to make you aware of a few other possibilities, and how best to handle them:

## Case Interviews

Case interviews are standard techniques to select candidates at consulting firms, business schools, software companies, banks, and customer service positions—in short, professional, collegial environments. In general, they come in three types and are designed to prove that you are, indeed, the creative and logical thinker your resume claims you are, or that you're the "people person" your recommenders claim you can be.

A key thing to remember with all three types is that there is no "right" answer to the case. They are behavioral tests that assess mental agility.

### Group Case Interviews

These are more about not failing than wowing people. They have one goal: to find out which people work and play well with others. Are you collegial and can you make an impact in a tactful way in a group setting? So while you definitely want to demonstrate that you can contribute, you don't want to dominate the group's discussion or attempt to take charge in an aggressive way. One of my clients had the experience of being in a group of eight people tasked with deciding whether an American chain restaurant should expand into Asia. They were given half an hour, a white board, and told to come up with a yes/no answer and a bulleted list explaining why. Of the eight, three failed. Two because they didn't speak and one because he couldn't stop telling everyone why his idea was right. If you are in this situation, I recommend the following techniques:

- Be the quiet organizer: suggest that everyone take the first four minutes to read the case and offer to keep time.
- Suggest something constructive or share any insights that you have.
- If you have no insights, ask people clarifying questions about their ideas.
- Be respectful of anything anyone else contributes, no matter what you may think of it.
- Follow the directions. (I know it seems insane that I have to write that, but experience has shown me I do. For example, if they say, "Only use what you've got," don't offer to look something up on your PDA.)

Bottom line: be a team player that contributes respectfully to the goal and you'll be fine.

## Individual Case Interviews

In these you CAN wow. But, again, it's not going to be because you got the right answer. Sometimes given in written form, and sometimes out loud, they range from "big thinking" questions (for example, one of my clients was asked what he would do about the environment if he were president of a country; his first clarifying question was "On earth as a whole or are we considering space exploration?"—at which point, he knew he had them) to brain teasers (another was asked why manhole covers were round—FYI, it's so cables don't get caught on any corners) to practical tasks. When confronted with these, keep the following in mind:

- Use all the time they give you.
- Make notes/use paper—particularly if it's orally delivered.
- If they say you can ask clarifying questions, do, but don't fish too much: show that you can be content working with the facts you have.
- As you lay out your answer, state your assumptions.
- Stay cool, even if you make a mistake in the arithmetic. All is not lost; they are looking at logic flow.

- Not all the information may by relevant, but don't say, "That's irrelevant." You may be wrong. If you think it is, just don't draw on it in your answer.

Again, the point is never that they are asking you the question because no one in their office can find out the answer—they want to see if you can think logically and clearly under pressure, making reasonable assumptions. Approach them like a doctor trying to figure out symptoms and you'll be fine. If you want to do more research, check out AcetheCase. com or QuintCareers.com/Case_Interviews.html.

If you're more in a movie mood, check out McKinsey.com/ Careers/How_Do_I_Apply/How_to_Do_Well_in_the_ Interview.aspx.

### Simulation Cases

For these you are likely being offered cases about the industry in which you'll be working. For customer service positions, they will test how you handle customer service complaints. For sales, they will give you a sample sales situation—for example, one of my clients was put in a room and asked to make three cold calls while being recorded. In these moments, a key thing to remember is not to joke about the situation or problem (I know it sounds obvious as you read it, but some people do relieve tension this way) and show that you can follow the rules and live up to whatever the company's values happen to be: if they stress customer satisfaction, make sure the customer is satisfied; if they stress efficiency, keep an eye on your time, etc. The US Postal Service has a great one for finding out if people can follow directions: they put everyone in a room, hand them a multiple-choice test, ask them to read the directions carefully, and not discuss the test among themselves. When the participants turn the test over the directions say "Please write your name and contact information in the blocks provided. DO NOT ANSWER ANY OF THE QUESTIONS BELOW OR WRITE ANYTHING ELSE ON THIS PAGE. Just wait five to ten minutes, and then turn the paper in as you leave." The trouble is, some people try to answer the questions and when they do, they fail, regardless of whether or not their answer was right. Why? Because the Post Office wants people who follow directions and only do what is written.

As you can see, there are many, many ways to handle these different scenarios. The most important things to remember throughout are prepare, remain calm, don't try to game the system, and be sure to thank everyone involved profusely upon leaving.

# ACE THE Q & A

I recognize that the majority of you have spent a considerable amount of time both preparing for and answering tough interview questions. That said, there remain a few that perennially stump my clients. With this in mind, I have included them—and their answers!—below, so you can be sure to field them like a pro.

Let's begin with the seeming innocuous "softball" (i.e., something so big you don't know what to swing at):

## *"Tell me about yourself . . ."*

Please note: This is not an opportunity to talk about your-self. Nobody wants to hear "I was born in Connecticut/I'm the youngest of six children/I went to X University." Instead, this is a chance to talk about what you will be contributing to the company once you are hired. So your answer should sound something like, "Your job description states you are looking for someone who can do X and Y. Not only can I do X and Y, I can also do Z."

## *What's Your Greatest Strength/Weakness?*

Almost everybody knows the importance of having an example in-hand for a question along the lines of "What's your greatest strength/weakness?" Or, "Tell me about a time when you made a mistake/solved a problem." The trouble is that this includes HR directors nationwide. Con-sequently, directors everywhere have begun to follow up their first request with, "That sounds great. Can you give me another example?"

Since they know you've prepped, let's out-prep them.

As you know, any example of your greatest weakness is just one of your strengths taken to an extreme: you're just so darn persistent, you don't know when to give up. Or, you're just so fascinated by your subject that you tend to want to include every detail, etc. If you're speaking about making a mistake or solving a problem, your focus is on the lesson you learned, or, as they say in HR-speak, "the fall that made it possible to stand." For example, "In retrospect, it's easy to see how a different choice would have been a better fit for the situation; the positive outcome, however, is that this reinforced the value of being accountable for my decisions, and showed me I have the stamina to regroup and rebuild when things don't go my way."

Now that you have those under your belt, let's look at how and why your round two answers should build on them:

First, you want to make it seem like their second request for an example surprised you, as it will make them feel far more sparkly and make your considered answer that much more effective—having a completely different, pat response might mean they tune you out or write you off. Given this, I recommend having your second response be an extension of your first. So, your second response to the query about your greatest weakness might sound like, "Well, when I think about being persistent, one thing I've learned is that if you're going to keep following up with a potential client you can't take rejection personally—in fact, it really helps to keep a sense of humor. For example, when I found myself calling this guy for the fifth time the other day, I prefaced it with, "Well, since this is my fifth call, I'm pretty sure we're going steady." If you were to tackle the "lesson learned," you might go with: "One thing I learned about coming back from a situation like that is that getting my team back on board—making sure I was accountable to them, and allowing them to offer me feedback—was as important as cleaning up the public outcome of my decision. Internal trust is as critical to success as external trust."

Having worked out the verbal elements of your answer, I recommend practicing every aspect of the interview with a friend. Yes, I understand it's excruciating—I, too, am not a fan of make-believe—but your delivery is as important as your answers. And in this particular case, if you jump right into your second response, it's going to seem canned. If you take a moment to think about it, it's more likely to be taken at face value.

Here's another example of what this might sound like:

HR DIRECTOR: *(looking down at your resume in an attempt to appear nonchalant)* "So, what do you think is your greatest weakness?"

YOU: *(after waiting until he or she looks back up at you)* "I'd have to say my greatest weakness is I sometimes I just don't know when to give up. When I identify an opportunity, I'm like a dog with a bone. This is why I like working with a team. Feedback helps me maintain my perspective."

HR DIRECTOR: "That's great. Can you give me another example?"

YOU: *(after pausing and seeming to consider)* "Well, speaking of teamwork, sometimes my energy can be a bit intimidating to people without my horsepower. I'm a fast thinker and speaker and I've learned I need to hold back sometimes—be more patient with the process. Since noticing this I've made a point of soliciting the opinions of the rest of the group before I move on to the next idea."

Now let's move on to the more exciting possibilities:

### "Are you overqualified?"

What your interviewer is really asking with this question is, "Are you going to leave in six months and make me look bad/waste the money we spent training you?" Your answer, then, must reassure them about your commitment: "I'm very excited about the position. I'm very passionate about working for your company—and once you hire me, I'm willing to make a minimum 18-month commitment to the job."

### "What can you contribute?"

If you are someone who has recently graduated from school, it's hard to differentiate yourself—you simply haven't had much experience. Given that, you need to talk about your "soft skills." So your answer would begin, "In addition to the work experience on my resume, I have a number of valuable soft skills." Follow that statement with examples that suit the situation. For example, if the company is all about staying late, you would say, " I have a strong work ethic—14 hour days aren't going to faze me." If the company is intensely private, "I understand, and value, discretion." If they've been having trouble with turnover, "Loyalty is a quality I value in others—and I'm very loyal myself," etc.

### "I just don't think you're right for this position."

Recently, interviewers have been stopping candidates mid-sentence and saying this—it's how they are weeding out indifferent candidates. If this happens to you, your response should be, "I'm sorry you have that impression—I must not be conveying how passionate I am about working with you. May I take you through my thinking one more time?" If you can smile when you say this that's even better.

Throughout your interview, you want to keep the following non-verbal elements in mind (as noted in *How to Wow*):

- You want to be sitting up and forward in your chair.
- You want to have your hands where your interviewer can see them. We trust you when we can see your hands—we don't trust you when we can't.
- You want to pause before answering each question, inhale, and speak on an exhalation to give your voice resonance and authority
- You don't want to begin speaking until the interviewer is looking at you, not at your resume.

Since you have them where you want them, you might as well enjoy it.

### "What's your current compensation?"

Another question people struggle with is "What's your current compensation?" and I agree this is a tricky one. Very few people are making what they want (or need) to earn, and they don't want to lowball themselves by talking about

that number. They also recognize they must not fib. (Ever.)
So, what to do?

My recommendation is to pull a "debating politician" strategy. In other words, answer the question you want to answer first.

Q: "What's your current compensation?"
A: "Well, I'm looking for a position that offers compensation in the range of $225K—more than I'm making right now, but also more in line with what I think I have to offer at this point in my career."

If they keep pushing: "My current compensation is lower than I'd like, which is part of why I'm looking for a new role."

And if they still keep pushing, it's possible you don't want to work for a boss who can't read cues. But if you do want to work for him, tell the truth. Lying is unacceptable, and continued evasiveness will make you seem untrustworthy.

# PRESENTING YOUR (CHECKERED) PAST

Very few of us have a life that has proceeded smoothly from point A to point B to point C. Whether you're fresh out of school, returning to the work force, coming back from a layoff, or switching industries, it's likely you have a moment or two in your past that take some explaining. With this in mind, I have included a few pointers for these conversations.

Before we look at these, however, a general note: regardless of the facts of your case, the tricky bit is to present the information to a potential employer in such a way that you don't sound like you'll be out the door just after they get you acclimated. Here's how I recommend proceeding:

If you're in the mood to get it over with, and your interviewer begins with "Where shall we start?" you could respond, "Well, if I were sitting where you're sitting I'd be concerned about the gaps in my resume, so why we don't we tackle them first?"

It's always better to be on offense than defense.

If you want to wait until things warm up a bit, you can wait for your interviewer to bring it up, at which point you can say, "I'm glad you asked me that."

So, let's begin:

### The Fresh Out of School Response

For many people, school was not necessarily a linear path, but instead included some time off, a wide variety of internships, or a fifth-year "victory lap." Here are a few ways to present this:

*The Time Off Response:* "Yes, I did take some time off and I'm so grateful because it's gotten my wanderlust out of my system. Without it, it's likely I would have abandoned a career shortly after starting it. Now I'm ready to give my career my full attention.

*The Multiple Internships Response:* "Yes, I have had a wide variety of internships. This has been great for me because it really helped me focus on what I want to do and don't want to do. I can now state unequivocally that X is where my heart lies."

*The Fifth Year Response:* "Yes, I did include a fifth year. This was because I realized halfway through that I had chosen the wrong major/wasn't giving my studies my full attention/needed more time to round out my resume. My fifth year gave me the opportunity to round out my education so I could bring my best to the workplace."

### The Returning to the Workplace Response

As noted earlier, you always want to begin with "I'm so glad you asked me that." In this case, you then segue to "As you can imagine, single parenthood/caring for an aging parent necessitated a great deal of time and attention. That said, my children are older now/my father's routine is stabilized, so those factors are no longer in play."

### The Multiple Past Jobs Response

If you've held a number of jobs because you had trouble settling on a career—or settling into the idea of working at all—you're going to need a slightly different response. In this instance, I would say, "As you can see, I've had the opportunity to try a number of different kinds of jobs, and I've learned a great deal from all of them—each provided skills that I was able to incorporate moving forward." I would then list the *very specific* reasons that brought you to the company. For example, "The reason I'm here today, however, is because I'm such a fan of your products/your values/your history."

## The Recently Laid Off Response

In this case, I highly recommend bringing it up at the outset, but in the following way: "As you can see, I was recently laid off from X company, which was not only highly disruptive, but very discouraging—I loved my job! Given that, I'd like to ask about your plans for growth/expansion in the next five years, as I don't want to find myself in this situation again anytime soon."

In every scenario, I would close with, "Once you hire me, I'm ready and willing to give the company 100%."

# ADVICE FOR "EXPERIENCED" JOB SEEKERS

Let's face it: if you're an "experienced" job seeker, this means you're often one of the older candidates—and being an older candidate can sometimes mean you make the person across from you very, very nervous.

Why? Well, he or she might think you'll leave should you get an offer that's more in line with your experience; they might worry that you don't have the requisite skill set; they might be concerned that you won't fit into the "vibe" of the office; they might be nervous about being in charge of someone who is their senior.

Luckily, the script below addresses all their concerns.

Before we look at what to say, however, let's look at when to say it: I recommend bringing it up at the outset of the interview (or during the "Do you have any questions for me?" portion of the programming.). The reason for this is they won't want to bring it up themselves (they don't want a lawsuit) but they're definitely thinking it.

Once it's on the table, I would say, "If I were sitting where you are sitting I would be wondering about whether or not my age is going to be a factor. I can tell you that I'm very committed to this company and this position. (This addresses their concern about you leaving should you get a better offer.) I have the requisite skill sets of a younger candidate (That takes care of that concern.), plus I have the invaluable soft skills that come with having been in the working world for 30 years: I'm quick to build camaraderie with my colleagues; I understand the importance of a strong work ethic; and I'm discreet." (All of which offsets their concern about you fitting in with the "vibe.") "Additionally, I've raised my family so you have my full attention." (Bonus points for you!)

The other critical piece is to organize how you look and sound while you say this. If you sound defensive, or if your body language shrieks that you're on high alert, this answer is not going to work. Keep it easy, keep it relaxed, keep it collegial. Breathe. Smile. Lean forward. Nod as you speak.

All of which assures them you're already on the same team.

# SURVIVING INTERVIEW DISASTERS: DON'T GET FLUSTERED, GET FACTUAL

Over the years, several of my clients have gotten questions/ been exposed to choices that left them, literally, speechless. And while I hope that all of you find yourself working together with interviewers who demonstrate consummate professionalism, I thought I'd pass along the following questions and situations, and my suggestions for responses, so you can see the importance of remaining factual when your interviewer gets freaky.

In the first instance, my client was an older candidate who was applying for a job in a youthful organization. During the course of the interview she was asked, "Do you know the average age of the people who work in this company?"

While we could only speculate about what the interviewer's intention might have been, I can tell you the result was my client was left feeling shamed for even applying.

How do I recommend you handle this kind of leading question?

Leading questions demand fact-based responses. You don't want to get into what you think your questioner is after, or do the dirty work of negating something that hasn't been overtly stated.

Consequently, my Monday-morning quarterbacking coaching to her was to simply have responded, "I do."

If you can smile when you say something like this, that's even better.

In the second instance, the interviewer said to my client, "You realize you're going to need to ugly-up if you get this job."

This leading question was asked of one of my, admittedly, extraordinarily beautiful clients. And, again, while we could only speculate about the questioner's intention we both found the pigtail-pulling undertone distinctly . . . underwhelming.

As ever, I don't want you to do your interviewer's dirty work for them. In this case, my 20/20 hindsight recommendation was to go with a factual, "I don't understand what you're saying."

As you can see, this puts the ball back in their court—and I promise you they will drop the ball.

Finally, one of my clients went into an interview during which, in her words, "The interviewer turned his back to me throughout the interview and asked his questions while looking out the window."

How did I recommend she handle it? Well, calling him on his behavior was going to end in a lose/lose. His reaction was unlikely to be positive, her outcome was therefore likely to be negative. Consequently, I suggested that she might have said, "I find it hard to answer your questions without being able to see your face. May I ask you to turn around, or may I join you at the window?"

What makes this statement powerful is that it takes the onus on herself—it's not that the interviewer is difficult, it's that it's tricky for her to talk to someone who refuses to look at her. Also, it reminds him that her goal is to be her best self in every situation, no matter how preposterous.

And, as I'm sure you've discovered, if you can be your best self—regardless of the circumstances—not only do you wow others, you wow yourself: the ultimate challenge.

# MANNERS MATTER

These days job interviews take all kinds of forms, among them business lunches and dinners. Generally the final round in a series of hurdles you've had to clear, these are less about assessing your business acumen—this has been solid enough to get you to the final round—than about seeing how you are able to interact with others in collegial and social situations. In short, this is where the smallest of small details is what separates those who receive an offer from those who receive a phone call saying, "I'm so sorry to have to tell you this—it was a really tough decision—but we've decided to go with someone else."

*How to Wow* covers the broad strokes of socializing with others: be on time, order food that's easy to manage, follow your host's lead with regard to beginning with small talk versus diving into a business conversation. Don't drink, don't discuss your dietary habits, don't say you've got to "hit the head." Since covering those basics, I've realized there are many more pitfalls than even I was aware were possible. Here's an example I heard from one of my clients. (Yes, it's true.)

As you know, multiple rounds of interviews are common in the financial industry. In this instance, the gentleman in question had met with a number of firm members and for this, his third, he'd been invited to have lunch at the local Chinese restaurant with the guys who'd make up his team. With everyone seated, an order was put in for a number of dishes that could be shared. Food began arriving and this gentleman—perhaps confusing his Chinese restaurant etiquette with his Japanese restaurant etiquette—reached into the basket of moo shoo pancakes, plucked one out and used it as a face towel.

It seems he didn't get the job.

While this may seem an extreme example, there are numerous ways—large and small—of knocking yourself out of the running for your dream job. Since I would hate to have any etiquette misstep undermine your hard work, here's a down-and-dirty list of things to know before your next meeting or lunch:

1. It seems insane that I have to put this in writing, but experience has proven I must. Wash your hair. Clean your nails. Do not chew gum. (Altoids are great to ensure fresh breath before you arrive, but they need to be gone before you go through the door). If you shave, shave properly, and that morning.

2. That cleanliness advisory given, I wouldn't recommend turning up smelling so strongly of scent that it lingers after you do.

3. Please do not wear your sunglasses, either on your face or on your head. Unless you're talking through the deal points of your new record contract at the Urth Café on Melrose (or a professional poker player), you look foolish.

4. Do not have MP3 player headphones hanging out or visible (much less in your ears). The same goes for wireless earpieces for your cell phone— take them off and put them away.

5. If you carry a briefcase, make sure that it isn't

overstuffed and chaotic looking: remove all candy wrappers, old sandwiches, etc.

6. While I have no objection to the flaunting of chest hair or cleavage on your own time, it needs to stay under wraps in a business setting. I would also recommend covering any tattoos you might have, at least until you get a sense of the environment or culture. The same goes for ankle bracelets and visible body piercings.

7. When arriving at or leaving the building, remember that you don't know who's on the elevator with you—or who might get on. Don't be the guy with the phone against his head yakking about what's just about to—or what just did—happen.

8. The same is true when you're in the Ladies' or Men's room. Again, as bizarre as it may seem that I have to write this down, office and restaurant bathrooms are not extensions of your home bathroom. This is not the time to make personal calls, do a complete makeup or wardrobe overhaul, or settle in with a magazine or book.

9. Political buttons, religious pins, Star Trek badges, etc., have their place, but not in inter-

views or on business occasions. No matter how committed you may be to a cause, these topics are potential minefields; best to keep your affiliation decorations for personal occasions.

10. Should you need to blow your nose during your interview or lunch, please excuse yourself to do so. If a sneeze catches you unaware—and unprepared with a handkerchief—please excuse yourself to wash your hands.

11. If they take you to a restaurant, you can be pretty sure that they're checking your table manners: now is not the time to order dishes that you adore but are hard to eat neatly. (Save spareribs and lobster for your celebratory lunch after you get the job.) In the same vein, don't be too picky or fussy about the food when presented with the menu—your primary objective is to make a good impression on your future employers, not show them that you are a gourmand (unless, of course, the job involves food).

12. Aside from the fact that my mother always impressed on me that salting your food before tasting it was an insult to the chef, I've heard that those in the business world view it as indicative of poor impulse con-

trol—you may make judgments without having all the facts.

13. Don't drink, even if they do.

14. Nobody—and I repeat nobody—is so important they need to check their PDA during an interview or lunch. The people with whom you're talking need to have 100% of your focus. If you can't give them this when you're sitting in front of them, why would they believe you will give them this when you aren't?

15. I would also request that you refrain from looking at it in between standing up from your table in the restaurant and exiting the door, or until you've left the building in which your meeting took place. You need to give your goodbyes the same attention you did your hellos.

16. Do not get in the elevator and begin calling your friends to discuss what occurred. I would also not recommend debriefing it within a two-block radius of the building or in any nearby restaurant. You don't know who's listening.

Alternatively, there are a number of things you can do that will contribute to your confidence, reassure others, or just flat knock me out with their fabulousness. Following a few of those:

1. Should you have to ring a doorbell or buzzer that someone answers (as opposed to "buzzing" you in), take one step back from the door after pressing the button for entry: you'll look better to the person answering the door at that distance.

2. As you know, when you step in from being out in the cold, it's almost always necessary to blow your nose. Knowing this, step into a nearby store, or arrive at the venue a few minutes early, and take care of this—repeated sniffing as you're being introduced is as hard on you as it is on those around you. *How to Wow* offered the rule of thumb "Two is one, and one is none": this is never more true than for handkerchiefs/Kleenex.

3. Conversely, if it's hot, leave extra time to get there so you're not rushed, and carry a handkerchief to clean up (i.e., mop your brow) before going in.

4. If you wear glasses, clean them thoroughly before going in. It helps you see, but it also helps others see your eyes, which builds trust (I know of one man who was offered a cloth to clean his glasses halfway through an interview

because the interviewer found them so distract-ingly smudged.)

While many of you are likely to have had the major-ity of this information at your fingertips, I'm hoping there were one or two things that were new information—or, at the very least, made you laugh. On that note, one of the greatest compliments you can offer your interviewer, or lunch partners, is your enthusiasm. Bearing the above in mind—and coupling it with genuine enthusiasm for becoming a part of the group—is sure to net you the offer you are looking for.

# THE SOCIAL INTERVIEW

As noted earlier, life is business and business is life, and every now and then life takes you to places you might not be super-comfortable—for example, if a networking acquaintance invites you to his private, social club, or a potential employer wants to see if you really are a good sport. With this in mind, here are a few dos and don'ts for attending the theater, symphony, or opera; meeting at someone's private club; or playing tennis or golf:

## At the Theatre, Symphony, or Opera

- Ask what others are wearing, and follow suit. If they are going to be in suits and ties/dresses, you need to be as well.
- A note on vocabulary: you go to *hear*, not to *see*, an Opera.
- Punctuality is *vital*. You will simply not be let in if you are five minutes late.
- When taking a seat in the center of an aisle, you always pass other people in that row facing them, not putting your backside in their face. If you are being passed, stand up if at all possible.
- Blinking lights mean get to your seats (AND turn off your phone).
- Don't overdo scent.
- Don't talk. No really: don't talk. Again: is you phone ringer off?
- Don't eat, drink, chew gum, etc.—you can eat and drink during intermission. If you can place drink orders before intermission, do.
- Avoid jingling jewelry and large hairstyles.
- Knowing when to clap can be tricky—technically, you should only do so at the end of scene or act. Watch others for clues.

- At the end, do not try to sneak out before the curtain calls: it is rude both to the audience and especially rude to the live performers who have just given their all for you. This applies to encores, too.

### At city and country clubs

- Check the dress code—it is likely to be quite "old fashioned." You can do this by asking your host or calling the club.
- As you enter, tell a member of the door staff your name and whom you are meeting. They will tell you where you can wait if your host is not there yet, and where to find your host if he or she arrived before you.
- If you do arrive before your host, stay in the waiting room to which you are directed. Other than the restroom, do not be tempted to wander or "look around."
- Never bring out business papers or work of any sort. If your host does not raise business topics in conversation, you shouldn't either.
- In general, speak 20% more softly than you are used to.

- Almost all clubs restrict use of cell phones—let your host be your guide, but plan on being out of contact electronically entirely while you are in the clubhouse.
- Never offer to pay, and you do not try to tip staff.
- If using the club's athletic facilities, make sure your shoes are clean before entering, be scrupulous about not hogging equipment, wiping down equipment after use, and putting things back where you found them. Avoid Neanderthal displays of grunting, "hydrating," etc. Do not be irritatingly competitive. Women should wear sports bras; men, jock straps.
- Always communicate with club staff through your host, not directly (e.g., your host asks waiters and waitresses to get refills for you—you don't order them from the club staff yourself unless your host invites you to do so.).
- Do not ask your host (or anyone else on the premises) about membership procedures, dues, who else is a member, etc. The history of the club or its building, however, are likely to be a welcome topic of conversation.

*On the tennis court*

- Wear whites. Even if they aren't deemed mandatory by the club's rule book, they're sure to look fresh and appropriate.
- Don't wear your hat backward or short shorts.
- Wear tennis sneakers (i.e., those with little or no treads). Sneakers of any other kind will tear up the clay or grass courts.
- Always let your host lead going on and off the court.
- Don't chatter during the game. You're there to play.
- If you're a great deal more accomplished than your host, tone down your game to your host's level, and compliment your host on the strong points of his game.

*On the golf course*

- Dress appropriately. If you are in doubt about anything, ask your host, or the facility where you will be playing. (Again, no backwards hats or short shorts. Women, Bermuda shorts and golf skirts should be just above the knee, no shorter.)
- A note on vocabulary: you are going to "play golf." You are not "golfing."

- Compliment your host on the facilities and condition of the course. Note how pleased you are to be playing a course you've always wanted to play.
- Stay out of a player's line of sight while they prepare to hit a shot. Don't walk in your opponent's line on the green, or make noise when he is putting.
- No one cares what your handicap is as long as you play fast.
- Let your host set the bet and the game.
- Be polite (and listen to) caddies: they know the club, players and rules far better than you do.
- It's a lovely gesture to offer to tip the caddies for yourself and your host. Your host will likely refuse, but if you insist, he will be grateful.
- Men should have a blazer in the car, and both men and women should have long pants, in case you are asked into the clubhouse for a meal.

No matter what the sport, it's important to be a good loser, and a gracious winner. Regardless of the outcome, shake your opponent's hand. Say, "Good game."

# CREATE CAMARADERIE

No matter how corporate a company's culture might be, it is still made up of people—and those people want to hire someone they can make small talk with in the elevator; someone they can imagine hanging out with at the local sandwich place; someone who will have their back in a meeting. With this in mind, here are a few things you can do during your interview to demonstrate the camaraderie you will bring to the office once you are hired.

*Pick three small-talk topics*

While it may seem pedantic, it's important to think through three potential topics for small talk prior to your arrival at the interview. What this does is smooth over transitional moments such as waiting for the elevator to arrive, or for the waiter to bring the menus—times which can be awkward if silent, or potentially deal-breaking if the topic you choose at random lands badly.

*Eat and drink what you're offered*

Lots of people worry about whether to accept an offer of water or coffee for fear of appearing difficult or demanding. In fact, accepting signals both your openness to your interviewer, and your feelings regarding a potentially positive outcome to the meeting. This doesn't mean that if you're offered coffee you say, "May I have a double no-fun, no-foam mochachino with six splendas." All that's necessary is, "Yes, thank you so much."

*Write down what people tell you*

Here's what I know: if people don't see you writing things down, they don't believe a) that you are interested in what they are saying or b) that you are going to remember what they have said. (If you doubt me, consider how you feel when the waiter doesn't write down your order in a restaurant—can you relax?) With this in mind, whether you use the notes or not, write down what others tell you.

Again, while none of the above is groundbreaking in and of itself, each contributes to an impression of a future colleague who won't be tongue-tied in the elevator; who is ready to be welcomed as a peer; and who will be detail-oriented enough to have your back in the next big meeting.

# THE POLISHED FOLLOW-UP

Most people know to send a thank you note after an interview, but few give their note the same time and attention they do their cover letter and resume.

This is a mistake. Your thank you note(s)—yes, that's plural—are a great way to differentiate yourself from other candidates.

First let's look at your email thank you note. While I do request it arrive within 12 hours, I am not impressed when it arrives within half an hour, as this leaves me thinking you just walked out to your car and typed it into your PDA. Even if you have established a certain "form" to your notes, the person receiving it should think you put some time into it.

So what is this form? There are at least three elements I would include.

Open with specific thanks. So instead of "Thanks for meeting me today," you might say, "It was a pleasure to meet you today. I enjoyed our conversation about X," and/ or, "I look forward to demonstrating my commitment to Y." This is an easy way to jog their memory if you are one of hundreds.

If you mentioned an industry-related book or article during your interview that you thought they'd enjoy, an email note is a great time to include a link to that; it's a "gift with purchase" for your interviewer.

I often have clients close with "I will plan to follow up with you in the next two weeks," rather than "I look forward to hearing from you," as I think it demonstrates confidence.

Now, for your snail mail note: Since I do want that to arrive within 24 hours, I recommend you bring a pre-addressed, pre-stamped envelope and several note cards with you to the interview and plan to write your note immediately upon leaving so you can drop it in the mailbox nearest your interviewer's office. When it's on their desk the next morning, trust me, they will be impressed.

If you are an uncertain speller, type your note into your PDA first to double-check your choices. If you are nervous about your handwriting, well, this is why you brought several note cards. Try, try again.

While it can be similar to your email note, they should not be identical.

Again, be specific regarding what you enjoyed learning about and how you see yourself contributing once you are hired.

If they made any mention of upcoming vacations/children or pets being under the weather/big presentations in their future, a nice way to close is with something along the lines of "I hope you enjoy your time in Aspen/that Rover is back to feeling his best/that you and your team knocked your presentation out of the park."

Demonstrating that you can communicate in two mediums, electronically and via the written word, is guaranteed to make you stand out from every other candidate.

# BE A GRACIOUS LOSER

Many of us are so devastated when we don't get the job that we can't think clearly—or don't wish to—about how we end the relationship we've had with our interviewer.

This is a mistake. I've gotten at least two jobs by being gracious and staying in touch. In one case, the person they hired ended up leaving within two weeks; in another, the gentleman who didn't hire me gave my name to his colleague down the hall.

So what do I recommend you do?

While it is hideously difficult for you, it is often difficult for your interviewer as well. With this in mind, I suggest saying something along the lines of, "I know these aren't easy calls to make and I want to thank you for speaking with me."

After that, if you're feeling strong-ish, you might say, "I do hope you will keep me in mind should other opportunities arise."

Finally—if it truly was your dream job—I recommend sending along a note a week or two later thanking them again for their time and consideration, and reiterating your hope that they will continue to keep you in mind moving forward.

As I've said, in my experience, it's astonishing how these small gestures pay off.

# DON'T BREAK YOUR OWN HEART

Swami Kripalvananda said, "My beloved child, break your heart no longer. Every time you judge yourself you break your own heart." I love this quote because I know how easy it is to get caught up in thinking how you could, or should, have done things differently. But if the way we talk to ourselves, about ourselves, is shaming, blaming, angry, destructive—pejorative in any way—how can we expect to show up in the world confident in our ability to contribute?

From what I've observed, the trouble often begins

when we begin comparing our insides to other people's outsides: a nasty mental cul de sac that can lead to an internal dialogue along the lines of "I can't believe I let that happen," "I'm such an idiot," or "how could I have been so blind?"

For example, I have one client who had worked with a public relations firm for the last ten years. For the two years before the firm declared chapter eleven, he had been hearing rumors of cost cutting on the employee level combined with the acquisition of still larger and more lavish houses and cars by the CEO. His trouble was that not only did my client like the guy at the top—he'd taken a chance on him when no one else would—he was also scared to move as he had a mortgage, credit card bills, school fees for his kids. . . . So he stayed. And when the firm did indeed go belly up, the death throes were compounded by my client's anger at himself for not leaving sooner. His brain became a non-stop feedback loop of self-loathing—which only added to his stress at having to look for a new job.

At this point, the request I made of him, and I would make of you, is to step back and ask yourself: would I speak to a close friend that way? My guess is you wouldn't. Or, as my friend Bill said to his girlfriend Sarah when she was running herself down, "Hey, don't talk about my girlfriend like that."

The tricky part is that, as the saying goes, familiarity breeds contempt. We're often so deep inside our own story, and consequently so conscious of all our mistakes, that we forget to give ourselves credit for all the kind, smart, or strategic things we do, instead choosing to focus on all the things we think we could or should be doing differently.

My point is that you do have a choice, and the more productive choice to make is to shift your focus from self-improvement to self-acceptance. I'm not saying it's easy, but I am saying it's possible.

This is not to say you get a bye on creative procrastination, heedless decisions, or generally poor behavior—these are never acceptable, and if you notice a pattern to their occurrence it needs to be addressed. What I am saying is that most of us are doing the best we can with the tools that we've got, and cutting ourselves some slack is going to get us further than beating ourselves up. Your willingness to think the best of yourself is going to help others think the best of you, and increasing your awareness of the story you tell yourself is the quickest way to have that story change.

We all deserve a great story.

With this in mind, I offer you the following:

When I first started my company—and please note this was career change number five—one of my advisors took me out to lunch and said, "Here's what nobody tells you: there's plenty of room at the top—so come on up."

That knocked me out. In a world where many successful people like to shroud their decision-making in mystery—preferring instead to make their good fortune seem inevitable to them and unattainable by you—finding someone willing to say, "Hey, when you're ready, there's more than enough to go around," was indescribably heartening.

And I promise when you believe this to be true—know on a cellular level that it is your right to be at the top—you will be.